GETTING TO KNOW
THE U.S. PRESIDENTS

HARRY S.
TRUMAN

THIRTY-THIRD PRESIDENT
1945 – 1953

WRITTEN AND ILLUSTRATED BY MIKE VENEZIA

CHILDREN'S PRESS
AN IMPRINT OF SCHOLASTIC INC.
NEW YORK   TORONTO   LONDON   AUCKLAND
MEXICO CITY   NEW DELHI   HONG KONG
DANBURY, CONNECTICUT

D1362087

Reading Consultant: Nanci R. Vargus, Ed.D., Assistant Professor, School of Education, University of Indianapolis

Historical Consultant: Marc J. Selverstone, Ph.D., Assistant Professor, Miller Center of Public Affairs, University of Virginia

Photographs © 2007: AP/Wide World Photos: 24; Corbis Images: 3, 17, 19, 20, 21, 29, 31 (Bettmann), 27 (Elio Ciol), 30 (Hulton-Deutsch Collection), 5 (Nagasaki Atomic Bomb Museum/epa), 28 (Abbie Rowe/National Park Services), 11, 15; Harry S. Truman Library and Museum: 12 (Hare Studios of Independence, MO), 16, 32.

Colorist for illustrations: Andrew Day

Library of Congress Cataloging-in-Publication Data

Venezia, Mike.
  Harry S. Truman / written and illustrated by Mike Venezia.
     p. cm. — (Getting to know the U.S. Presidents)
  ISBN-13: 978-0-516-22637-8 (lib. bdg.)   978-0-531-17946-8 (pbk.)
  ISBN-10: 0-516-22637-1 (lib. bdg.)   0-531-17946-X (pbk.)
  1. Truman, Harry S., 1884-1972—Juvenile literature. 2.
Presidents—United States—Biography—Juvenile literature. I. Title.
II. Series.

  E814.V46 2007
  973.918092—dc22
  [B]

                                    2006023365

2 3 4 5 6 7 8 9 10 R 17 16 15 14 13 12 11 10

Harry S. Truman was the thirty-third president of the United States. He was born in his family's home in Lamar, Missouri, in 1884. As president, Harry Truman had to try to solve some of the scariest and most complicated problems of almost any president.

When President Franklin Roosevelt died suddenly on April 12, 1945, Vice President Harry Truman took over the job of president of the United States. Right away, Harry Truman was faced with one of the toughest decisions of his life. In April 1945, World War II was finishing up in Europe, but was still raging on in Japan.

In order to end the war with Japan quickly and save American lives, President Truman agreed to use a horrible new secret weapon called the atomic bomb. After the Japanese cities of Hiroshima and Nagasaki were destroyed by A-bombs, the Japanese surrendered.

The United States dropped an atomic bomb on Nagasaki, Japan, on August 9, 1945.

Even though hundreds of thousands of people died, President Truman truly believed many more people on both sides would have been killed if the war had gone on any longer.

When the war ended, President Truman realized his next huge problem would be dealing with Communist Russia. At that time, Russia controlled a union of republics known as the Soviet Union. The Russians, who had been friends, or allies, of the United States during the war, began taking over countries in Eastern Europe. Communism is a system in which the government controls the social and economic lives of its citizens. The government collects food and goods that workers produce. Then the government is supposed to hand out those things so that everyone gets equal amounts.

Communist governments didn't want anyone to be too rich or too poor. They believed people would be better off if no one had more than anyone else. Unfortunately, anyone who disagreed with the government could be thrown in prison. President Truman was definitely against Communism. He worked hard to stop it from spreading to free, democratic countries.

On top of everything else, President Truman had to help the United States get back to normal after the war. When millions of soldiers returned home from overseas, they needed jobs and homes right away. There were shortages of all kinds, though, from houses and washing machines to toasters and cars.

The problem was that it took time for factories to change back from making wartime products to making everyday products again. When people couldn't get what they wanted, they began to blame President Truman for not making things happen fast enough.

While Harry Truman was growing up, his father worked as a horse trader and farmer. Mr. Truman often brought young Harry to work with him. Horse trading was a rough, tough business. Harry learned lots of bad language from the horse traders. Later, Harry Truman was known to use colorful language to make a point, even when he was president.

Harry Truman (right) at age four with his younger brother Vivian

Harry and his brother Vivian and sister Mary Jane moved with their parents to a few different farming areas in Missouri. They finally ended up in the city of Independence.

Harry Truman at about age thirteen

When Harry was six years old, he found out he couldn't see very well. Harry had to wear thick glasses. His mother didn't want him to roughhouse or play sports. Harry then became interested in other activities. He started taking piano lessons. For excitement, he read every book he could get his hands on.

Harry especially loved history and adventure books. By the time he was a teenager, Harry said he had read every book in the Independence library. All that reading helped Harry become a very good student.

Growing up, Harry Truman had trouble making friends. He was shorter than almost everyone else his age. He was the only one in his class who wore glasses. He didn't play sports, and he avoided fights. Harry got picked on a lot by other kids.

World War I soldier
Harry Truman

When Harry entered high school, things got better. Harry made new friends and joined clubs. He hoped to go to college, but his parents didn't have the money. Plus, Harry's father needed him to help out on the farm. Harry hated farming but worked on the farm until the United States entered World War I. In 1918, Harry went overseas to fight in France. During the war, Harry was promoted to captain.

After the war, Harry Truman (left) opened a men's clothing store.

Harry discovered he was a pretty good leader. Even though he was small, he was tough. His men respected him and were thankful for his wise decisions in battle. Soon after he returned home, Harry married his childhood sweetheart, Bess Wallace. Bess and Harry had one child, Margaret. Harry also started up a men's clothing store.

Harry Truman with his wife, Bess, and daughter, Margaret

At first, the store was pretty successful. Then, after the whole country went through some hard times called a recession, the store went out of business. It was then that Harry thought he would try getting into politics. When Harry was growing up, his father had taken him along to Democratic political meetings. Harry had always loved the excitement he found there.

Democratic leaders had noticed Harry Truman. They knew he was super-honest and had been a good leader during the war. They asked Harry to run in the next election for county judge. County judges were responsible for collecting taxes and raising money to pave roads and build public buildings.

Roads in Missouri at the time were in terrible shape. Harry promised to fix them up. Harry won the election. He kept his promise, too. Harry was a judge for most of the next twelve years. In 1934, Harry's Democratic friends thought he should run for U.S. Senator. Harry's reputation for being honest and hard working helped him win that election, too.

Senator Harry Truman at home in Missouri with his family

When Harry Truman traveled to Washington, D.C., with Bess and Margaret, the United States was going through one of its toughest periods. The country was in the middle of a terrible economic depression. This meant that many people had lost their jobs and companies were going out of business. Some people even lost their homes.

In Europe in 1939, a German dictator named Adolf Hitler and his armies began to invade and take over many nearby countries.

German dictator Adolf Hitler in 1939

The United States entered World War II when Japan launched a surprise attack on the American naval base at Pearl Harbor, Hawaii, on December 7, 1941.

Then, on December 7, 1941, Japanese fighter planes attacked America's naval base in Pearl Harbor, Hawaii. The United States declared war on Japan. These events were the beginning of World War II, the world's most destructive war.

In 1941, Senator Truman was put in charge of a special committee. He was responsible for making sure the billions of dollars spent on defense weren't being wasted or stolen by greedy companies. Senator Truman found there was a lot of waste going on. The Truman Committee did everything it could to stop crooked manufacturers and get rid of lazy workers.

Senator Truman was furious that anyone would cheat the government during a war. He personally investigated companies and army bases. He used his talent for colorful language whenever he found anything dishonest going on.

Truman (left) has lunch with President Franklin D. Roosevelt (right) after being chosen as FDR's running mate in 1944.

President Roosevelt really appreciated the job Senator Truman was doing. When Roosevelt decided to run for a fourth term, he asked Harry Truman to be his vice president. Only a few months after the election, however, President Roosevelt died.

Just like that, Harry Truman became president of the United States. After he made his decision about dropping the atomic bomb, President Truman began finding ways to return the United States to peacetime.

To stop Communism, President Truman declared the United States would help any country that was in danger of being taken over by a Communist government.

Russia was just as determined to spread Communism as the United States was to stop it. Soon, the Cold War began. It was called the Cold War because its main participants, the United States and the Soviet Union, fought each other with words and threats rather than weapons and military action. The public was jittery anyway, though. Many people panicked, thinking there were Russian spies all over the place.

Soon, government agencies were set up to investigate suspicious citizens. There were, in fact, some Communist spies in the United States, but many innocent people were accused of wrongdoing. Some people got in trouble for even knowing Communists. This event was known as the Red Scare. The favorite color of Communist nations was red. Their flags, symbols, and banners were red or had red backgrounds. Red has often been used as the color of revolution.

A military parade in the Soviet Union during the Communist era

In an effort to win a second term, President Truman traveled across the country on an old-fashioned "whistle-stop tour" by train, speaking at every stop.

In 1948, when it was time for the next presidential election, Harry Truman was very unpopular. No one thought he had a chance of winning. Harry surprised everyone, though. He worked harder than ever, giving speeches all over the country to convince people he would make the best president.

The *Chicago Tribune* was so sure Harry's opponent, Thomas Dewey, would win, that before all the election results were in, they printed a story saying that Dewey had won. Harry Truman had the last laugh, though. He ended up being re-elected!

Harry Truman laughs as he holds up the newspaper that incorrectly predicted the outcome of the 1948 presidential election.

U.S. troops on a muddy road during the war in Korea

During President Truman's second term, the Cold War began to heat up in Asia. In 1950, Communist forces from North Korea invaded South Korea. South Korea was on friendly terms with the United States, so Harry Truman didn't hesitate to send American soldiers to help the South Koreans. Some people disagreed with the president's decision. They were afraid it might start another world war.

General Douglas
MacArthur

People also disagreed with the president when he fired the general in charge of the American and allied forces in Korea. General Douglas MacArthur was a super-popular World War II hero. General MacArthur stopped obeying President Truman's orders, though, which was a very serious offense. Even so, people all over the United States were angry with Harry Truman for dumping their favorite general.

President Truman had a famous sign on his desk that said "The buck stops here!" He thought it was the president's job to make decisions and take responsibility for those decisions.

In 1952, Harry Truman decided not to run for president again. When he left office, he was one of the most unpopular presidents in history. Years later, though, people have realized Harry Truman's tough, common-sense decisions were usually right. Today, Harry Truman is considered to have been one of the best presidents ever. Harry Truman died on December 26, 1972, at the ripe old age of eighty-eight.